Love

Collection

You Must Love Me

Wise Publications
London / New York / Paris / Sydney / Copenhagen / Madrid

Exclusive Distributors:

Music Sales Limited
8/9 Frith Street
London W1V 5TZ
England.

Music Sales Pty Limited
120 Rothschild Avenue
Rosebery, NSW 2018
Australia.

Order No. AM944339
ISBN 0-7119-6615-X
This book © Copyright 1997
by Wise Publications

Cover designed by CDT Design

Compiled by Peter Evans

Printed in the United Kingdom
by Staples Printers Rochester Ltd.,
Rochester, Kent.

Cover photograph courtesy of
Paul Bradforth

Your Guarantee of Quality

As publishers, we strive to
produce every book to the highest
commercial standards. This book has
been carefully designed to minimise
awkward page turns and to make
playing from it a real pleasure.
Particular care has been given to
specifying acid-free, neutral-sized
paper made from pulps which
have not been elemental chlorine
bleached. This pulp is from farmed
sustainable forests and was
produced with special regard for
the environment. Throughout, the
printing and binding have been
planned to ensure a sturdy, attractive
publication which should give years
of enjoyment. If your copy fails to
meet our high standards, please
inform us and we will gladly
replace it.

Music Sales' complete catalogue
describes thousands of titles and
is available in full colour sections
by subject, direct from Music Sales
Limited. Please state your areas of
interest and send a cheque/postal
order for £1.50 for postage to:
Music Sales Limited, Newmarket
Road, Bury St. Edmunds,
Suffolk IP33 3YB.

Visit the Internet Music Shop at
http://www.musicsales.co.uk

Contents

And I Love Her

Words & Music by John Lennon & Paul McCartney

1. I give her all ____ my love, ____
2. She gives me ev - 'ry - thing ____
3. Bright are the stars ____ that shine, ____

that's all I do. _____ And if you saw ____
and ten - der - ly. _____ The kiss my lov -
dark is the sky. _____ I know this love ____

my love \
-er brings \
of mine

you'd love her too.____ \
she brings to me.____ \
will nev-er die.____

I____ love \
And I love \
And I love

To Coda ⊕

| 1 | 2 |

_her._____ \
_her._____ \
_her._____

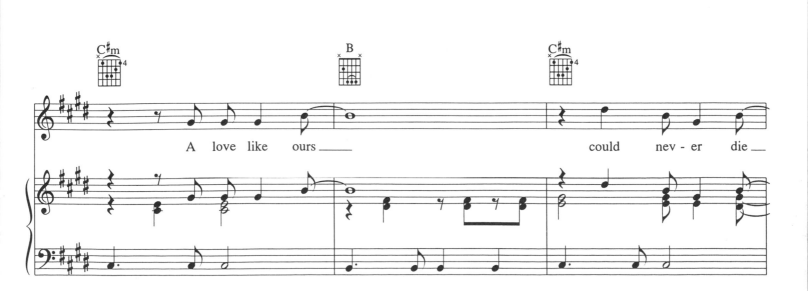

A love like ours____ could nev-er die____

will nev-er die. ___ And I love ___

her. ___

Candle On The Water

(from Walt Disney Pictures' "Pete's Dragon")

Words & Music by Al Kasha & Joel Hirschhorn

Don't Let Go (Love)

Words & Music by Ivan Matias, Andrea Martin,
Marqueze Etheridge & Organized Noize

15

Don't You Love Me

Words & Music by Cynthia Biggs, Carolyn Mitchell,
Terence Dudley & Christopher Kellum

Child goes to the store for a loaf of bread,— don't you love me,— don't you

Verse 2:
Vicki's Granny has to walk the streets,
Don't you love me, don't you love me no more.
Tryin' to find herself a place to sleep,
Don't you love me, don't you love me no more.
See the cops arrest another kid,
Don't you love me, don't you love me no more.
Mother's crying don't know where he is,
Don't you love me, don't you love me no more.

Feel Like Making Love

Words & Music by Eugene McDaniels

Endless Love

Words & Music by Lionel Richie

I Believe

Words & Music by Ervin Drake, Irvin Graham, Jimmy Shirl & Al Stillman

Moderately (with much expression)

I Be - lieve for ev - 'ry drop of rain that falls, ___ a flow - er grows. ___ I Be - lieve that some where in the dark - est night, ___ a can - dle glows. ___

I'll Be Your Baby Tonight

Words & Music by Bob Dylan

If I Never See You Again

Words & Music by Graham Lyle/Terry Britten/Marti Pellow/Graeme Clark

-ly   I'm touched by your love._____   Ev-en if I nev-er see you a-gain.

if I nev-er see you, if_____ I nev-er see you a-gain,   oh,_____

_____   and if I nev-er see_____ you a-gain,_____   oh._____

No- one can tell you how the sto-ry ends_____   where the

Verse 2:
The night is so unforgiving,
And I'm all on my own.
I realise what I'm missing,
And now that you've gone.
So I say a prayer,
And you up there,
Are you feeling what I'm feeling now?

If I never see you again *etc.*

One Sweet Day

Words & Music by Mariah Carey, Walter Afanasieff,
Shawn Stockman, Michael McCary, Nathan Morris & Wanya Morris

heav-en, _____ like so man-y friends we've lost a-long the way. _____ And I

know e-ven-tu-al-ly we'll be to-geth-er _____ one sweet day. _____

And I _____ Sor-ry I nev-er told _

you _____ all I want-ed to say. _____

Laughter In The Rain

Words & Music by Neil Sedaka & Philip Cody

Lovin' You

Words & Music by Minnie Riperton & Richard Rudolph

Lov - - in' you_____ is ea - sy 'cause you're beau - ti - ful,

49

Something's Gotten Hold Of My Heart

Words & Music by Roger Cook & Roger Greenaway

(1.4.) Some-thing's got-ten hold of my heart __ keep-ing my soul __ and my sen-ses a - part.__
(2.3.) Some-thing's got-ten hold of my hand __ dragg-ing my soul __ to a beau-ti - ful land.__

(1.3.)
(2.4.) (Yeah __)

Some-thing's got-ten in - to my life __ cut - ting its
Some-thing's has in - va-ded my night __ paint-ing my

way through my dreams like a knife.
sleep with a col-our so bright.

Turn-ing me up, _____ turn-ing me down,
Chang-ing the grey, _____ chang-ing the blue,

mak-ing me smile, _____ and mak-ing me _____ frown.
scar-let for me _____ and scar-let for _____

1.

In a world that was small, _____ I once lived in a time _____

that was peace with no trou-ble at all. _____ But then you came my

1° only

% only

But then you, you, you, you came my

Somewhere Out There

Words & Music by James Horner, Barry Mann & Cynthia Weil

57

The Wind Beneath My Wings

Words & Music by Jeff Silbar & Larry Henley

It must have been cold_ there_ in my shad - ow,

to nev - er have sun - light on your face.

You've been con - tent_ to let me shine,

truth:

I would be noth-

in' with-out you.

D. S. % al Coda

wings.

You are the wind

be-neath my wings.

Up Where We Belong

Words & Music by Jack Nitzsche, Will Jennings & Buffy Sainte Marie

When I Need You

Words & Music by Albert Hammond & Carole Bayer Sager

Moderately, with feeling

You Are Not Alone

Words & Music by Robert Kelly

and leave my world— so cold?— (1, 3.) Ev-'ry

day I sit— and ask— my-self— how did this thing end?—

Some-thing whis-pers in— my ear— and says.— (2. 4.) You are not— a-lone—

but you are not— a-lone— lone,— lone,—

Verse 2:
You are not alone
I am here with you
Though you're far away
I am here to stay.
You are not alone
I am here with you
Though we're far apart
You're always in my heart.
But you are not alone.

Verse 3:
Just the other night
I thought I heard you cry
Asking me to go
And hold you in my arms.
I can hear your breaths
Your burdens I will bear
But first I need you here
Then forever can begin.

Verse 4:
You are not alone
I am here with you
Though you're far away
I am here to stay.
But you are not alone
I am here with you
Though we're far apart
You're always in my heart.
But you are not alone.

You Must Love Me

Music by Andrew Lloyd Webber
Lyrics by Tim Rice

1. Where do we go from here? This isn't where we in-
(Verse 2 see block lyric)

tend-ed to be. We had it all, you be-lieved in me, I be-

Verse 2: (Instrumental 8 bars)
Why are you at my side?
How can I be any use to you now?
Give me a chance and I'll let you see how
Nothing has changed.
Deep in my heart I'm concealing
Things that I'm longing to say,
Scared to confess what I'm feeling
Frightened you'll slip away,
You must love me.